LightBearer

The Soul's Journey In Astrology

Written and Illustrated by

SHARON RUSSELL

PINK MOMENT PRESS

Published in the United States of America by
Pink Moment Press
Submit all inquiries at www.sharonrussellart.com

Library of Congress: 2014949649
ISBN: 978-0-9825000-9-5

Illustrations by Sharon Russell
Book design by Suzy Bennitt and Sharon Russell

10 9 8 7 6 5 4 3 2 2016 2015 2014

made with love
in Ojai, California

Know Thyself

Foreword

There are many books about astrology on the market today, but none can offer what Sharon Russell has created by painting the feminine essence of each of the signs of the zodiac. You are all twelve of these archetypes; they each make up some area of your life or personality. Sharon explains how each sign relates to and is an outgrowth of the one before it. Her descriptions will help you to relate to this embodied science which describes the personality of the Self in a very different way than the ancient symbols of crabs, scorpions, fish, goats and lions.

I have been an astrologer for forty-six years studying, giving readings and teaching how this first human science can help others reach their full potential. The old symbols of astrology lacked feeling and beauty, two important aspects of the feminine nature. There was a certain kind of hidden meaning in the animals, humans and things they represented but connecting them to something I could embody and relate to on a daily basis was not possible for me.

Thirty years into astrology I began to wonder if my talented sister Sharon would recreate these symbols into the feminine images. It didn't take much more than a nudge as she was already having ideas and images of women for paintings, not realizing that they fit the astrological archetypes. Our minds may learn through words, symbols, and life experiences, but our hearts learn through beauty and feelings. We are not made of mind alone. We have an eternal Soul that learns by feeling and being drawn into the irresistible world of beauty, of nature, of engaging fully with life.

Let your life be a challenge. Trust that it can unfold in mysterious ways, living and breathing the fullness of life that your astrological chart speaks of. Let the signs that Sharon has created in a human and passionate way help you learn and stay centered in the dramas that touch your life. They can bring a new awareness that will awaken you to your personal journey. Like the woman in the painting, they are the KEY that will unlock the full potential and amazing individual that you are meant to be.

Yours Lovingly,

Dixie Gladstone

Dixie Gladstone
feminineastrology.com

Bridging Differences

Throughout my life I have desired to find ways to bridge differences between people, their opposing ideas, as well as the conflicting ideas within myself. As a child, and even still, people arguing and having different opinions has always been hard for me. It has meant the possibility of ending love or connection, winner - loser, right - wrong, dominator - victim. One way of looking at this issue is that it is our undeveloped, unevolved archetypal energies that create these struggles within ourselves or with others.

I believe these differing energies come from the one power (God, or for others Goddess, the Higher Power). They work along a continuum from less skillful to very skillful. Archetypes can become stagnant, repressed, projected onto others (let your husband be the skeptic), be ignored, played out irresponsibly or responsibly. From ancient times to the present we have developed a stronger sense of who we are, allowing us to become more the orchestrator of our life, rather than be taken over by urges or uncontrolled, unevolved desires - archetypes. At this point in our evolution we have the potential for shifting the orchestration from purely Ego to a Wiser part of ourself.

Using the images of Kuan Yin and Mother Mary, a kind of East meets West, different religions, philosophies, politics, cultures, values, and customs are symbolically facing one another. And yet with all these differences there also exits a place of connection. Both these energies are Mothers who embody Compassion and want to alleviate or lesson the sorrows of the world. This can be an idea for ourselves to explore: where do different archetypes have a similarity that can be met, dance together rather than fight or disagree?

Introduction

This art book is designed to draw you in with your visual senses and then to help you understand the various archetypal energies that live within you and want to be awakened so you can receive their gifts and allow them to evolve. Carl Jung, the psychologist who mentored with Freud, coined the word "archetype" meaning patterns or roles that people play. We have a mother archetype, father, teacher, adventurer, skeptic, lover, etc. Most of us rely heavily on two or three.

I have created an image of a tiger to represent our INSTINCTUAL NATURE which exists in our unconscious. Our instincts are vital to our survival. We have many instincts starting with the basics of physical survival such as fulfilling needs of hunger, sex, sleep and aggression. Instincts are the basis for the structures and patterns which form our behavior. I think of them as similar to archetypes, that is, the root of what becomes an archetype. An ARCHETYPE adds to the patterns and behaviors of the instincts a visual IMAGE. This could be an image of our various roles such as trickster, warrior, hero, priest, etc. Instincts are inherited patterns that are not innately good or bad; they order our psyche.

The woman in the picture is gently approaching the tiger because she wants to learn to interact more skillfully with this energy, allowing her to do more than just survive, but also thrive. Instead of coming from instinct alone, we can add the dimension of conscious participation with our Self, so we can more fully express what has been gifted to us. Our individual experiences and possibly DNA (nature and nurture) color in each archetype differently from one person to another. To one person the warrior archetype may mean a violent person, a murderer, but to someone else the warrior could mean a protector, someone you appreciate and respect.

Being around different people will bring out different archetypal energies inside of you and at different stages in your life different archetypes will awaken. Sometimes

Making Friends with Your Instincts

we connect to the standard age related life passages such as the student when we are young and in college, or the mother when we become pregnant. But awakening to archetypes within us isn't always related to being young, middle-aged or retired. We all have heard of people unsuccessful in business when young only to blossom when everyone else retires. And of course there are women who are motherly and never had children or students who were just surfing in college.

I have found it can be helpful to know a bit about astrology to better understand why we function well or not so well during different Life Passages, for astrology shows you your basic personality type as well as timing. You may be born with no energy in the 3rd or 9th houses of your astrology chart, or no planets in Gemini or Sagittarius, or a poorly aspected Mercury. These aspects are all related to learning, being a student or teacher, sharing ideas. Years later you might have a Transit with an outer planet moving through your 9th house and this could awaken your desire to become a serious student.

People have different coping styles. Some people get bigger, some smaller. You can do either in a constructive or destructive fashion. You can get bigger through being assertive, standing up for yourself, or you can get bigger by being aggressive, being a persecutor, winning at any cost. You can get smaller by feeling sad, stepping back, reflecting on your feelings, a positive thing to do, or by feeling depressed, or as a form of manipulation. It is all possible.

These different coping styles, strategies, patterns are found in the archetypes. Their styles can bring us blessings and be our gifts as well as be the source of our problems when they are used in extreme or at inappropriate times. It is not always the problem that is the problem but often the response, the coping style, the gift used out of balance that needs to be addressed.

Let us look for a moment at the water sign of PISCES. It has a gift of caring, being receptive, and wanting connection which can evolve into compassion. When these traits are used as a coping mechanism when under STRESS, you might find yourself giving in to another, trying to help them while they are abusing you. On the other hand you could step back from the situation and experience true compassion for a person because you see the fear that is behind their actions, yet not allow the abuse to continue, which may mean you stop helping them or help them differently.

You don't need to believe in astrology to benefit from this excursion or know anything about it. The twelve astrology signs give us information about basic archetypal energy and psychological understanding. Dates for beginnings and endings of signs can vary one or two days depending on the year of birth, so checking an Ephermeris will give you the exact day. We each have all the signs and planets somewhere in our birth chart. Our Birth or Natal chart is always who we are. And, as time moves on the planets move into different signs and houses. This gives us the opportunity to expand who we are and learn new skills, new ways of thinking. This is why it can be helpful to let yourself be drawn to any sign whether it is your Sun, Moon or Ascendent (Rising).

My sister Dixie, lover of women's groups and goddess myths, inspired me to do all the signs in feminine images rather than the traditional alternating of signs such as male Aries, female Taurus, etc. So bear with me as you view the images, and even the use of a female lion instead of the ram for Aries. I call it artistic license.

With Love and Light,

Sharon Russell

Sharon Russell
Author and Artist

An Invitation

As you read this book you may find it helpful to meditate on a certain image that you are especially drawn to or want to experience more fully. A simple meditation is to put a hand over your heart and breath slowly until you feel balanced and calm. Now take yourself back in time to a memory when you felt happy, loved, appreciated or cared for and re-experience that memory. As much as possible, remember smells, color or sound - whatever you can recall that is positive.

Now look at the illustration again - be with it and ask yourself a question such as "help me to learn more about how to have a successful business (Capricorn)." Or use the Affirmation on the bottom of the page "I enjoy blazing new trails as I develop my courage and follow the light of my fire (Aries)." After the affirmation, be still and breath slowly and deeply and listen. Insights may come now or anytime later. Patience is key.

I have portrayed the Soul going through the signs in their order as it does create a meaningful sequence and story. If you were born with your sun in Aquarius it does not necessarily mean you are more evolved than a Gemini, for each sign has it's more evolved and less evolved aspects. Since this journey isn't necessarily linear, you may find yourself going back to certain images over and over again or skipping around. You might focus on an archetype you don't know very much about and work on developing this energy, or you might try to incorporate the positive qualities of a sign you are very familiar with in its less skillful form. Journaling your thoughts after being with an image is another way to access a deeper connection with yourself.

March 20 to April 19

ARIES ~ TrailBlazer

Stepping out into the landscape of life, your Soul awakens to the call for adventure, to new beginnings and new possibilities. The fiery pioneering energy of Aries gives you courage, boldness and passion as you open yourself to your instinct for survival, all of which you can use to become a TRAILBLAZER.

You are meant to have an independent nature and develop a strong sense of self and self-will. As you awaken your will, you discover, like a leafy green sprout pushing through the earth toward the light, the ability to struggle valiantly for what you want to attain and become. This doesn't mean that you don't ever experience fear but that you can learn to "feel the fear and do it anyway," because that is how courage and bravery are developed.

The call of Aries is "don't just sit there, do something" -- anything to get yourself started. Along the Aries road you can learn the difference between being assertive vs being aggressive, for fire can create energy, warmth and excitement or burn and destroy what is around it. Assertive, action-oriented Aries energy can make inspiring athletes, warriors and leaders for a cause, to be first or win as you prove your strength and receive recognition.

Let your spontaneous and instinctive nature show you the way as you pick up the flag and lead the parade. Your pioneering Aries archetype achieves success as you learn how to finish projects or delegate them to others, for you are learning what to do, how much to do, and when to stop.

AFFIRMATION

I enjoy blazing new trails as I develop my courage
and follow the light of my fire.

April 20 to May 20

TAURUS ~ Prosperity

After Aries fiery entrance into the landscape of life, your Soul now tries to carve out some comfort, security and relaxation through earthy Taurus. Here your sensuous Taurean nature finds a beautiful and peaceful meadow to relax amidst the flowers, delicious food, and the good things of life that cater to your five senses.

The sight of nature's rich velvety green grasses and colorful flowers, the earthy smells, the feel of soft silks and gentle breezes caressing your skin, the taste of succulent fruits and good wine, the sound of wind blowing through your hair or harmonious music all can be like a soothing balm to your Taurus archetype.

Perceiving and enjoying beauty in its many forms is the major gift you can receive from Taurus. Some Taureans desire to create wealth so they can own beautiful things or create a sense of security while others satisfy these needs for beauty through nature as in a sunset, rainbow, the mountains or a trip to an art museum. Taurus holds the secret of finding spirit in matter. Your Taurus archetype usually enjoys a few close loyal friends rather than many come and go friends.

Determined, persistent and stubborn, Taureans know how to hold on and keep going until the fruits of your labor ripen. Then you must learn when to let go and let God. Self-sufficient and often artistic, your Taurus nature expects the universe to be abundant and bring you PROSPERITY. The sign Taurus tells you a lot about what you value in life by where you spend your money and time.

AFFIRMATION

I am grateful for all the beauty and abundance in my life.
I know that I am prosperous.

GEMINI ~ Learning Tree

After bathing in beauty, comfort and security, your Soul is now restless and curious for new experiences and mental stimulation. Gemini's sign of the twins expresses the idea of a dual nature and rules the Law of Opposites, the rational conscious mind and the mystery of the higher self or super conscious mind. The mythology of this sign stems from the twin brothers Castor and Pollux -- one was the heavenly twin and the other was his earthly brother. The image of THE LEARNING TREE shows this twin nature taking in information, then releasing it to others.

Let your curiosity for the new open you to gathering information, thoughts and ideas, sorting and organizing, then sharing with others. It must have been a Gemini who said "if you want to learn something, teach it" for Gemini's make great teachers as well as networkers and sales people.

Aries initiates physical action, Taurus is contained and tenacious, while Gemini is adaptable and changes through learning new things and having an open mind. Called the "butterfly of the zodiac," your Gemini Soul can be found flitting from one situation to another, seeking some form of communication. You may find reading is your Gemini path, or writing, talking, or all of the above. When your Soul is illuminating the Gemini archetype, fast talking, quick responses, seeking the answers allows you to experience many points of view.

As your Gemini energy matures, so does your ability to slow down, listen compassionately and stay in one direction longer while distilling your past storehouse of information into a deeper wisdom of life.

AFFIRMATION

I enjoy stimulating conversation as I share and exchange ideas with others.

CANCER ~ Nurture

Your Soul has now had many varied experiences of awakening into this world starting with fiery pioneering Aries, then moving inward into practical Taurus seeking comfort and security, followed by Gemini moving outward to explore ideas while enjoying mental stimulation. The pattern continues and you will see that in this next sign of Cancer you move inward once again, seeking protection, security and comfort, a similarity to Taurus.

This emotionally sensitive water sign is strongly linked to domesticity and nurturing in its many forms. It rules the breasts, stomach, womb, the home, the interior of all things for it is the protective covering principle. Its symbol the crab is covered by its shell - home, which it carries on its back so it can retreat safely whenever it feels threatened. And similarly, your Soul will retreat home when in Cancer's realm and senses the need for protection. Spending time by the ocean or other bodies of water is soothing to your Cancerian archetype.

In the world of Cancer, you discover the importance of kindness, a gentle nature and learn about the different ways to NURTURE -- being able to Mother and protect the innocent, those in need. Most Cancers love to nurture their children and friends even pets and plants and need to make sure they don't forget to nurture themselves. Other Cancerians may expect to be nurtured and find it hard to give this energy outward. When you are on the road of Cancer you live in your feelings and affections and have a tenacious hold on those you love, and like Taurus, are learning when to hold on and when to let go.

The restless tides of the ocean reflect Cancer's ability to be changeable -- happy one moment, sad the next. You will discover that this energy is like a psychic sponge picking up whatever energy is around, hence the importance of staying out of negative situations or relationships as much as you can. Your intuition and psychic nature becomes more reliable as you learn to take good care of yourself and listen without fear.

AFFIRMATION

I nurture myself and others in a balanced way.

July 23 to August 22

LEO ~ Lady of the Sun

What is life without creativity and fun? Now that you feel nurtured and safe, it is time to let your dramatic and entertaining Leo out to play. The symbols for this shining archetype are the Sun, THE LADY OF THE SUN, the lion, king, queen, your inner and outer children. Your Leo nature has dignity, self respect and like the lion in the "Yellow Brick Road," has the gift of courage. As your Soul enters the very magical, colorful and fragrant garden of Leo, allow the sun to touch your heart and open you to the fires of passion, affection and joy. Fiery and romantic Leo rules the heart and matters of the heart and you want to be appreciated for your big heart and magnanimous efforts.

Your Soul yearns to be entertained, feel young, to play and enjoy the moment as children do, unselfconsciously. It's time to allow your inner comedian or dramatic performer to step out onto the stage and into the spotlight, to see life as a game worth playing. Didn't someone once say (and it could have been a Leo) that "life is but a stage and we are the performers?" Following your joy, your bliss, what makes you smile or laugh wholeheartedly will open your tremendous reserves of creativity and allow you to shine. Sometimes as a Leo you may find yourself shrinking because you don't feel acknowledged, appreciated or loved. This can be a sign that it is time to become a bit more detached to the outcome of your efforts. Don't worry about doing it perfectly or for the applause, do it because you can and it is fun.

As you allow yourself to be seen, your heart can open you to return the applause back to others. As your Soul begins to learn when it has been in the spotlight long enough, you can step off the stage and encourage another to enjoy the limelight.

AFFIRMATION

*I feel vibrant and playful as I open my heart
and allow my creativity to shine.*

VIRGO ~ Harvest

It's time now to get serious and practical after all that fun and enthusiasm in Leo. The call now for your Soul is service and a willingness to go through the effort of disciplining your self as you develop the ability to hone a craft and learn all the details necessary for a job well done. The earth sign of Virgo wants to pull all the frayed ends of life together, a daunting task to say the least. Along this road you learn the importance of not taking on more than you can chew. For if that happens, Virgo's analytical mind could get stuck and degenerate into fault finding, a paralyzingly perfectionism, or just give up.

Yet this perfectionism is important for your development. Your laser-like focusing ability will be able to pinpoint where the acupuncture needle goes, how to thread the eye of the needle, which bolts go where on the space ship. In other words, there are many tasks and jobs that require this kind of accuracy and attention to detail. Your somewhat shy yet grounded earth archetype of Virgo is learning to work hard and steady, developing patience quietly and thoroughly.

There is a similarity here with analytical Gemini as both use your rational mind to collect information. But rather than talk about it, Virgos want to assimilate information and turn it into a useful step by step routine, job, skill or craft while working quietly behind the scenes. Virgo's symbol is the gatherer of wheat whose efforts bring The HARVEST.

In the evolution of this sign you may discover that the chaos in the outer world that you are trying to order and perfect is a reflection of the chaos inside of you. Then you may learn how to find the place of ease in your mind within the efforting of life.

AFFIRMATION

I find the place of ease within this task.

September 23 to October 22

LIBRA ~ The Lovers

Charming and with a strong sense of justice and fair play, the intellectual air sign of Libra seeks connection with others especially through partnership or marriage. Libra will awaken your Soul's heart to become THE LOVER, for what would an incarnation be without the desire to come together with others? It is time now to move from me-ness to we-ness.

Ruled by the feminine planet Venus, goddess of love, the sign of Libra itself is masculine. Here you can see duality, opposites, dissonance and harmony in relationship, war and peace. The Libran dilemma is to learn to be cooperative and diplomatic without being self-effacing or opportunistic. Peace at any price ultimately won't work. The scales of balance is Libra's symbol for bridging opposing interests or points of view. The key for your Libra nature is ultimately win-win rather than win-lose, for if I win and you lose, I also lose -- in closeness and trust with you. But before you learn this kind of interaction with others your relationships may be more war-like than peaceful and loving. And yet even hostilities are a form of relationship. In recent years psychology has coined the term "co-dependency" which means being overly involved with another. How will you know if you are a co-dependent? Well, here is a thought that can help you understand this idea: If you find yourself falling overboard from a ship into the ocean, someone else's life will flash before you!

Libra will open your Soul's heart, mind and eyes to beauty in its many forms, a similarity to Taurus as both are ruled by the goddess of love and beauty, Venus. The key for this journey is using beauty and nature to release tensions and create a more serene inner landscape.

AFFIRMATION

I seek balance and harmony as
I open my heart and connect with others.

SCORPIO ~ Passion

In the water sign of Scorpio your Soul doesn't just want commitment or partnership with another as Libra does, here, you also want a deep, passionate and intense relationship that will unwittingly take you into your and the other's unconscious. In this process of exploration and curiosity you will discover their shadow, warts and ugly parts. If you hang in there long enough you will also discover your unpleasant parts, and hopefully Beauty in both Beasts and Gold in both Shadows.

This deep need for understanding helps you transform jealousy, vindictiveness and fear into love; anger and PASSION into compassion. Transformation is the key word for Scorpio as seen through its three symbols. The first symbol for this archetype is your raw instinctual nature found in serpents, dragons, the scorpion with its ability to sting itself and others. The second is the eagle able to fly high above the situation, the earth and get a better picture of what is going on, to see a bigger truth and get closer to Spirit. The third is the alchemical phoenix, a mythological bird who dies in its fire and is reborn from its own ashes.

Superficiality doesn't work for your Scorpio archetype because this intense energy takes you down the road of mysteries, the mystery of birth, death, rebirth, sexual union, money ~ yours and others, the shadow, any topic that is considered taboo by your culture. Along this road you may become interested in research that will give you answers to things that are hidden, such as psychology, astrology, the occult, science, medicine, healing, discovering your inner detective. Your strong willpower and emotional desires give you the tenacity to move forward discovering light in the dark murky waters of Scorpio, heights in the depths, self in the not-self as you unconsciously strive to understand a reverence for existence.

AFFIRMATION

I open myself to find the gold in everyone's shadow.

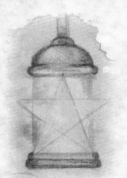

November 22 to December 21

SAGITTARIUS ~ LightBearer

The partnership energy in Libra and Scorpio and the attention to detail in Virgo has now opened your Soul's desire for a more light-filled and expansive adventure. There is a need for travel either through mind and/or body as you experience the optimistic and friendly fire sign of Sagittarius, for it is searching to find and understand the meaning of life. Through traveling in body, going to different countries, experiencing different religions, politics, and cultures, there is the possibility of learning to accept ideas unfamiliar to you and possibly different from your family of origin.

Sagittarius can use its enthusiastic energy in the world of sports, for in this arena your body can travel, not be confined. Some Sagittarians travel through their minds mostly, by reading, getting a higher education or fulfilling their need for understanding the value of laws by becoming lawyers, politicians, religious leaders. As you evolve you see the difference between man made and higher laws. When you learn that freedom is an inner state of mind rather than an outer condition, it will be easier for you to stay committed with people and projects.

Sometimes on this quest you may feel that life seems meaningless, pointless, that there is no bigger picture. You discover at different times in your life what is true seems to change, for the truth of a five year old is not the same as a 60 year old. As your Soul learns how to keep an open mind, truth will keep expanding you until you are able to allow others to have the freedom of thought that you so crave for yourself. The quest for adventure, the joy of discovery finally leads your Soul to awaken to the meaning that lies within your own self. This is when you arrive back home after your long journey and really know it for the first time. Others follow you, for you are the LIGHTBEARER of the zodiac.

AFFIRMATION

As I expand my vision, I find tolerance
and a deeper meaning on my quest for truth.

December 22 to January 19

CAPRICORN ~ Mastery

At this point your Soul is now asked to pull your expansive, freedom loving, search for meaning into a more focused and practical form that will bring your dreams into concrete reality. In the earth sign of Capricorn, the desire for MASTERY in the world pushes you to reach that goal no matter how long or how many setbacks you may experience. Material ambition gives you the ability to keep putting one foot in front of the other which will bring the success and admiration your Soul craves.

Here the journey seems to be more about the outcome, the goal rather than enjoying or being with the process. But don't let that stop you from learning to enjoy the process. In Capricorn you may ignore your emotional needs, perhaps even family or friends in order to create a successful career or business. As a Capricorn you could create friendships through work or even work with family members so as not to spread your own life too thin. Self-discipline and self-control can give you the results you are looking to create in the world, and if you are not appreciated or admired for all your hard work, you could pull back from work and become depressed. The other possibility is that you may isolate from others by doing more work, moving into the realm of workaholism.

In this responsible archetype you take your duties seriously and often become a person of authority, someone out in the public's eye. Tradition, established ways of doing things that have proved to be beneficial are important to you. Yet many Capricorn's develop a sense of humor to cope with all this seriousness. Mature Capricorn energy is rewarded in many ways as the potential for being rooted in heaven as well as earth awaits you at the summit.

AFFIRMATION

With a sense of humor and self discipline, I bring my dreams into reality.

January 20 to February 18

AQUARIUS ~ Community

The often traditional and reliable sign of Capricorn is now ready to move into a more progressive world of ideas as your Soul seeks freedom and authenticity in Aquarius. You can use your inventive, innovative maverick mind by stepping out of the box and daring to be different. Let the rebel part of you take a stand to help humanity. Join a group to save the whales and know there is a cost for this kind of authenticity. You are often the first to see the need for radical change in business, politics, institutions -- your energy is visionary and future oriented.

Here the Soul dances to a different drummer and is not cut out to follow established society. Something you have in common with another air sign, Libra, is the need for fairness and equality. The desire to be progressive shows up in trying to enlighten the world or your COMMUNITY to new ideas and also in the way you express yourself and/or dress. You may express your originality through your hair, piercings, clothing in an eccentric or even contrary manner and that may serve you, or it may not. Many Aquarians sincerely use politics and revolution to help humanity while others go through stages as they become aware of unconscious self-serving and ego-enhancing needs.

As an Aquarian you are friendly and optimistic because you believe in treating others as equals, however, you may fear the restrictions that occur in committed relationships. Commitment is easier in personal relationships when your partner understands your need for freedom and time spent in groups that have meaning to you - and vice versa. As your Aquarian nature evolves you learn what needs to be preserved, what needs to change as well as what is corrupt and needs to be overthrown.

AFFIRMATION

I open myself to friendly optimism to inspire needed change.

PISCES ~ *Serenity*

After experiencing a sense of Aquarian freedom from the constraints of Capricorn's focused earth reality, your Soul longs to merge with a greater whole. In Pisces, you as an individual, like a single falling raindrop, can have a sense of uniting with the sea. It is time now for your Soul to drink of Pisces waters and let yourself dream; then, if grounded enough from your Capricorn experience, bring your dream into this reality. This archetype needs a daily dose of Pisces vastness, reverie, ability to space out, stare out the window and, with a sense of SERENITY, drink in the beauty of this world. Your Piscean nature seeks peace, wholeness and often develops gifts of compassion and healing.

A sensitive often psychic water sign (as are all three water signs), intuitive and dreamy, Pisces slips you into the space of the poet, artist, musician, or dancer. You are learning all the ways of merging. Not only can you merge through the many different art forms mentioned above, you can also merge through nature, prayer, meditation or ritual. This archetype gives the gift of letting walls and boundaries melt, opening yourself to connection with others and the universe. Becoming aware of ways of merging that do not serve your best interest such as irresponsible use of drugs, alcohol, television, food and codependent relating is part of Pisces learning. This gentle water sign seeks to live in this world of duality and pressure and yet merge without escaping.

In the beginning of this journey of the wheel, your Soul was creating an ego and boundaries in order to take care of yourself, learn to relate to others and develop skills in the physical world. Now in the last sign you prepare yourself to let go of your ego, knowing that you can't let go of it before you have done the work of creating one.

AFFIRMATION

As I walk through healing waters returning to my true home,
I find peace and serenity.

Remember...

To Play ...
To Nurture Yourself and Others

Acknowledgements

So many people have helped me along my way to create this book. I would especially like to thank my wonderful husband of many years, Joe Zorskie, for being supportive and helping me with my computer - technological difficulties. Special thanks goes to my SOUL SISTER, Dixie Gladstone, for inspiring me to do my art, for helping me with her ideas and reading my notes along with putting me on her very creative website, feminineastrology.com.

I love the two women's groups that I belong to that show up to help promote my art, gift wrap my books and bring food, yes, you Linda Gray. And for their years of encouraging support and friendship, always being there, thanks to Elizabeth Spring, Terry Royce and Diane Jaffe.

This book would never have happened without my dear friend, Suzy Bennitt, who also inspired me to do my first book, a dragon story, "Innocence to Wholeness: Journey of the Heroine." Her artistic layout and design abilities are incredible. Suzy and her husband, Bob, graciously published this book with their company, Pink Moment Press, and Pace Marketing Communications.

Sharon Russell

Soul Sisters

About the Artist

Sharon Russell has lived in Ojai, California since 1983 and began painting her feminine watercolor art in 1999 during a period of illness and depression. Her first images were sold as cards and prints and eventually became the 12 astrological pieces you see in this book, followed by a Dragon Story also in 12 pictures. These images of the archetypal feminine have an uplifting and inspiring message which helped her move through her difficult time. The words for both books came during and after the art was created.

Sharon grew up in northern Oregon with her two younger sisters, brother, lumberjack father and mother from New York City. Her mother supplied Sharon and her sisters with an endless quantity of paper, crayons, pencils and coloring books to entertain themselves during the often rainy days in Oregon.

After graduating from Cal State long Beach in Art, Sharon worked for over 10 years in graphic design in Los Angeles, then later studied Transpersonal and Jungian Psychology and became a psychotherapist in Ojai for 15 years. Her timeless mythological art is featured on femineastrology.com, a website created by her sister, Dixie Gladstone and can be bought in card form or prints. You can also see Sharon on YouTube by searching: "Sharon Russell Ojai Artist."

SharonRussellArt.com
sharonrussell64@gmail.com

Made in the USA
San Bernardino, CA
09 May 2016